Click It

COMPUTER FUN

Writing

By Lisa Trumbauer

The Millbrook Press
Brookfield, Connecticut

Produced by 17th Street Productions,
33 West 17th Street
New York, NY 10011

Editor, Liesa Abrams
Cover illustration by Sam Ward
Interior design and illustrations by Sydney Wright

Library of Congress Cataloging-in-Publication Data

Trumbauer, Lisa, 1963-
      Click it! Computer fun writing / by Lisa Trumbauer; illustrated by Sidney Wright.
                  p.   cm.
      Summary: Briefly explains the nature of a computer, describes how to use a word-processing program to
create and save your writing, and suggests activities to develop use of language, good sentence structure, and effective
storytelling.
      ISBN 0-7613-1654-X (lib. bdg.). — ISBN 0-7613-1289-7 (pbk.)
      1. English language—Composition and exercises—Computer-assisted instruction—Juvenile literature.
2. English language—Composition and exercises—Study and teaching (Primary)—Juvenile literature. [1. English—
Composition and exercises. 2. Creative Writing. 3. Computers.] I. Title: Computer fun writing. II. Title.
LB1528.T78   2000
372.62'3—dc21   99-045542

1 3 5 7 9 10 8 6 4 2

CONTENTS

Now What?!

What's the sense of becoming an expert on the computer and learning a **word-processing** program if you don't show off your writing skills? With the activities in this book, you'll be a whiz on your computer and you'll also master the art of writing!

Why Writing?

Writing is one of the most useful skills you can develop. Understanding how to choose words carefully and how to put sentences together meaningfully will help you in everything you do. Writing is not only necessary but also a lot of fun—you can let your imagination go wild! The activities in this book will turn you into a writing expert. You'll learn lots of new words and find out how to use them in sentences. You'll even get to write a newspaper article, a poem, and a story with a setting and characters that you create yourself!

But since this is a *computer* book, you have to know some of the basics first. Here's your computer, inside and out:

What it is: You know that big screen that looks like a TV? That's the **monitor**.
What it does: It shows you what you're working on.

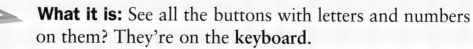

What it is: See all the buttons with letters and numbers on them? They're on the **keyboard**.

What it does: Here's where you type in what you want the computer to do and also all the words you want to appear on the screen.

What it is: Can you find the funky-looking curvy tool with one or two big buttons on it? That's the **mouse**.

What it does: It lets you move around the computer screen and choose where you want to go. How? Simple—once you understand some mouse lingo:

Cursor: This shows you where you are on the computer screen. Depending on which program you're in, it may look like a blinking line, an arrow, or an icon. In the **Paint** program, you can move the cursor by moving the mouse.

Click: When the instructions tell you to "click," you push the left button on the mouse and then release it quickly.

Drag: When you need to "drag" the cursor across the screen, you hold down the left button on the mouse and move it across the **mouse pad** it's resting on.

Write On

For the activities in this book, you'll need to understand how to use the **word-processing** program. That's what you use for writing, like when you want to write notes to a friend or make up a story about all your wild adventures as captain of a spaceship. Many different **word-processing** programs are available, but one of the most popular is **Microsoft Works**. The following activities are based on this program, but you can do them with any other program that your computer has. Here are some tips on how to use **Microsoft Works**:

Click on the word **Start** at the bottom of your computer screen. See that list of words above it? Move your mouse up until the word **Programs** is highlighted, then move your mouse to the right and you'll see the names of all your computer's programs. Look for **Microsoft Works**. Found it? Great! Click on it once, and then you'll see three choices. Click **Works Tools** once, then **Word Processor** once. Easy enough, right? Now you should have a blank screen, just waiting for you to fill it up with your writing!

At the top of the screen you'll see some words. This is called the **Menu Bar**. Move your mouse to one of these words, and an arrow will appear. Click, and you'll get a list with more words, called **commands**. You use them to tell your computer what to do. Here are the commands you will use:

- In **File:** Save, Page Setup, and Print
- In **Edit:** Cut, Copy, and Paste
- In **Insert:** ClipArt, Drawing, and Object
- In **Format:** Font and Style

Below the **Menu Bar** you will see a row of small pictures. This is the **Tool Bar**. The **Tool Bar** lets you do some things without using a command. For example:

- **Font Box:** This is the first thing you see on the left. It tells you the name of the type style, or font, that you are using. You can choose a new font (**FONT**, font, **font**, *font*) by clicking the arrow to see your choices, then clicking on the one you want.

- **Numbers:** These numbers tell you the size of your type. Click on the arrow to see how large or small you can make the type—small, normal, huge!

- **B I U:** These three boxes let you change the way the type looks.

   B stands for boldface. It makes the type **darker**.
   I stands for italics. It makes the type *slanted*.
   U stands for underline. It draws a line <u>under the type.</u>

- **Lines:** You might see three or four boxes with straight lines in them. These let you move the words you type to different parts of the screen. You can choose to put them all the way to the left, in the middle (centered), all the way to the right, or all lined up on both sides (justified).

Before you begin to type, choose a font and a size. You can do this on the **Tool Bar** by clicking a new font or type size. You can also do this by clicking **Format**, then clicking **Font and Style**. Here you will see fonts and sizes and **colors!** Choose a color, just as you would a font or a size—by clicking the arrow beside the **Color Box** to see the choices, then clicking the color once. When you've made all your choices, click the **OK** button to return to the main screen.

So now you're an expert at the writing stuff. What else is there? Painting! Did you know you could be a master artist without picking up a single paintbrush? You can actually paint pictures on your computer! Since you'll be doing a lot of that in the activities in this book, here's a guide to your **Paint** program:

Click on the word **Start** at the bottom of your screen. Remember this list? Click on **Programs** again, but this time choose the word **Accessories**. Yes, there's *another* list of choices. See the word **Paint**? You guessed it—that's where you click!

Whoa! Look at all your paint tools! And colors! Here's what some of the tools in the **Tool Box** can do:

- Pencil: draws a line
- Paintbrush: paints a thicker line
- Paint Can: fills an object with color
- Spray-Paint Can: makes splotchy, star bursts of color
- "A" Icon: makes a box for you to type in
- Shapes: these make exact shapes
- Dotted-Line Box: can move or delete art or type
- Eraser: erases color

To change a color, just click the color you want in the **Paint Box**. If you click the **Paint Box** twice, you'll get a grid with even more colors!

HINT!

Okay, we know the pictures you paint will be totally amazing, but just in case you want to sneak in some of the stuff by the pros, here's how to do it: ClipArt. These are pictures that have already been drawn and are stored inside your computer. In your word-processing program click Insert, then ClipArt. You'll see pictures of all kinds of things, from flowers to people to computers! Click the arrows to move the list up and down to see them. (This is called scrolling.) Then click once on the picture you want. A box will appear around it. Click the Insert button. The picture will appear on your word-processing page! The clip art in this book comes from sources other than Microsoft Works, and you can always buy software that contains more clip art!

PSST!

Exit the Paint program by clicking the box with the X in the upper-right corner.

Now that you know how to write and draw on the computer, there are only two more things to learn before you get started on the *fun* part—the activities! What good would your work be if you couldn't show it off to people? How do you do it? Easy—**Save** and **Print**.

Saving

Click on the word **File** at the top of the screen, then click **Save**. A box called **Save As** will appear. This box may have some folders in it. **Folders** are where the documents you save are kept. Choose a folder to keep your work in, or create a new folder. At the top of the **Save As** box, you'll see a folder with a star beside it. Click it once. In the box that appears, type the name you want to use for your folder over the highlighted words **New Folder**. Then hit the **Enter** key twice, which will open up your new folder. Type the name of your document in the white box that says **File Name**. Click the **Save** button. Your work has been saved!

Once you've saved your file, you'll want to print it out (see below) or start a new one. Click into **File**, then **New** to start a new page. Your old art will disappear, and a new, clean canvas will take its place. To open the file again, click **File**, then **Open**. Click on the name of your file once, and click the **Open** button again. Your work will appear!

Now Print!

You'll have to print out your "paintings" to put together mobiles, posters, and other projects. It would be best if you had a color printer. If not, don't worry!

1. Click **File**, then **Print**.

2. A box with print choices will come on the screen. Some of the activities in this book work better if you choose to print your page in the **Landscape** format. When you need to do that, the instructions will explain how. Otherwise just click **OK**, and your page will print.

That Should Do It!

The activities in this book are based on Windows 95, using **Microsoft Works** and the **Paint** program. Many versions of **Microsoft Works** exist, so yours might be a little different, or you may have a different **word-processing** or drawing program. You may have to alter the instructions slightly to fit your computer. Also, the pictures show how a finished product *may* look. Don't worry if your art looks a bit different. It probably will! That's because you used *your* ideas and *your* computer!

Computers can do all sorts of things, and you're about to see that for yourself. Your computer will be a big help as you explore the world of writing. Experiment by playing around with the words and by choosing different fonts, sizes, and colors. Be creative, and have a blast!

Chapter One

WORD POWER

Just as numbers are a basic part of everything you do in math, words are basic to everything you do in writing. These activities will show you how to increase your word power and, thus, your writing power.

 **WRITING** ## DESCRIBE IT

Adjectives are words that describe things. When you tell your friend about a bug that scared you, you don't just say it was a bug; you say it was a *huge* bug. That makes it easier for your friend to picture the bug. The more words you use to describe the bug, the more your friend can imagine what it looked like. It's like painting a picture with words. Once you've explained that it was a huge, black, hairy bug, he'll be screaming right along with you!

Steps:

1 Go into the **word-processing** program. Think of something you want to describe; for example, an object in your room that you really like. What words could you use to describe it? Think of the object's color, its shape, and its size. What does it feel like? Does it have a smell? What makes that object different from other objects? Think of as many appropriate adjectives as you can.

2 Type each word on a separate line. (Hit the **Enter** key after each word. You might want to hit the key twice to give yourself extra space.) You can type your words in different fonts, sizes, and colors too. Click **Format**, then **Font and Style**. Play around with all the choices until you find ones that you like. If you want, you can also center the words on the page so that there is space on both sides of the words. Click **Format**, then **Paragraph**. Look for the word **Alignment**. Below that word, there should be choices. Click the circle next to the word **Center**.

3 When you've typed all the descriptive words you can think of, type in the name of the object you're describing on the last line. Then **Save** all your words and **Print** them out.

4 Now cut the words out of the paper so that you have lots of scraps of paper with a word on each one. With a sharpened pencil, poke holes in each scrap of paper.

5 Get some yarn or string. Tie your words together in a long train. Once all the adjective words are tied together, attach the paper with the object on it to the end of the train of paper. See the art below for help.

6 Make more adjective trains and hang them all in your room.

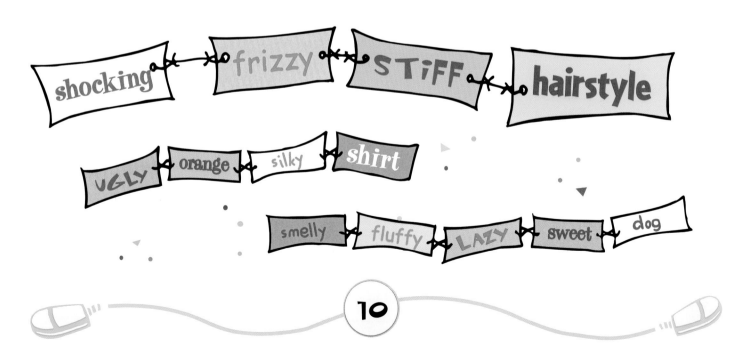

When you read a poem, the words sound nice together. Like stories, poems tell you about an event, a person, or a feeling. The difference is that most poems have a special pattern in the way they are written. Also, the words at the end of the lines often rhyme. Try writing a short poem using words that rhyme.

Steps:

1 Go into your **word-processing** program. One pattern that is used in poetry is called the *abab* pattern. That means every other line rhymes. The first line is an *a* line, and so is the third, so they have to rhyme. The second and fourth lines are *b* lines, so they have to rhyme. Here's an example:

2 You can use any of the sample rhyming words in the box below right, or think of your own! Just remember to match up the first line with the third line and the second line with the fourth line.

A Yesterday I went to school,
B and the teacher gave a test!
A I didn't study like a fool,
B and so I didn't do my best.

3 Don't forget to **Save** your poem and **Print** it out.

4 Now try illustrating your poem. Go into the **Paint** program, and use the **Paint** tools to draw a picture that goes with your poem. **Save** your picture and **Print** it out.

cat	eye	friend	steal
rat	lie	end	feel
sat	why	send	real
fat	cry	mend	meal

5 Get a shoe-box lid. Glue your poem and picture inside the lid. The edges of the lid will be like a frame around your poem and drawing! Stand the shoe-box lid on a bookshelf so that everyone can see your illustrated poem.

 **AS SWEET AS PIE**

You've probably heard this expression before. There's a name for such expressions—they're called *similes*. Similes compare things and use the words *like* or *as*. Comparisons can help you learn more about whatever is being described. For instance, when someone says that a person is "as sweet as pie," it means that the person is *very* sweet. You know that because you know that pie is very sweet! If someone says that a person "moves like a turtle," it means that the person walks very slowly! Learn more about similes as you make some riddle cards for your friends.

Steps:

1 Go into your **word-processing** program. Type the paragraph below onto your screen.

School's Out for Snow!

When two feet of snow fell overnight, the next day was a holiday. The streets were **as white as a new sheet of paper,** and the trees looked like ice-cream cones. School was closed for a week! We were as happy as dogs with new bones. We bundled up in tons of clothing, looking like creatures about to set off into space. We gathered our sleds and took off like race cars down a track, zooming down the hill. We rode as fast as the wind. When we got to the bottom, we charged back up the hill to do it all over. We looked like powdered-sugar doughnuts because we were so covered with snow. But we didn't care! We were as carefree as birds on a spring day. School was out, and we had snow! What more could we want?

2 Now read through the paragraph and find all the similes. We already found the first one for you! Each time you find one, highlight it by placing the cursor at the beginning of the phrase, then dragging the cursor across the whole phrase. Once the simile is highlighted, make it bold by clicking the **B** in the **Tool Bar** at the top of your screen. Here's a hint—there are eight similes in the paragraph, including the one we marked. Remember that a simile is a comparison using the words *like* or *as*!

3 **Save** and **Print** your word-processing page.

4 Now that you're comfortable finding similes, try to think of some yourself. Here are some to get you started:

- as busy as a bee
- as wise as an owl
- as happy as clams
- as stiff as a board

- as sly as a fox
- swim like a fish
- sing like a bird
- as bright as a star

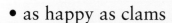

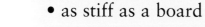

5 Use these examples and other similes you think of to make simile riddle cards. Go into the **Paint** program. Click on the **A icon** to make a text box. Type in one of the similes, like "as busy as a bee." Make sure the type is at least 20-point size, and leave plenty of space between the second *as* and *a*.

AS BUSY AS A BEE

6 Under the words *a bee* use the **Paint** tools to draw a picture of a bee.

7 **Save** your work and **Print** it out.

8 Now cut your phrase in half. On one piece of paper you should have the words *as busy as*. On the other piece you should have the words *a bee* and the picture of the bee. Get a piece of construction paper, and fold it in half, like a card. Glue the first part of the phrase on the outside front cover of the card. Glue the rest of the phrase, along with the picture, inside the card.

9 Show your simile card to a friend or someone in your family. Have them guess the picture and the words inside. Make more riddle cards for other similes!

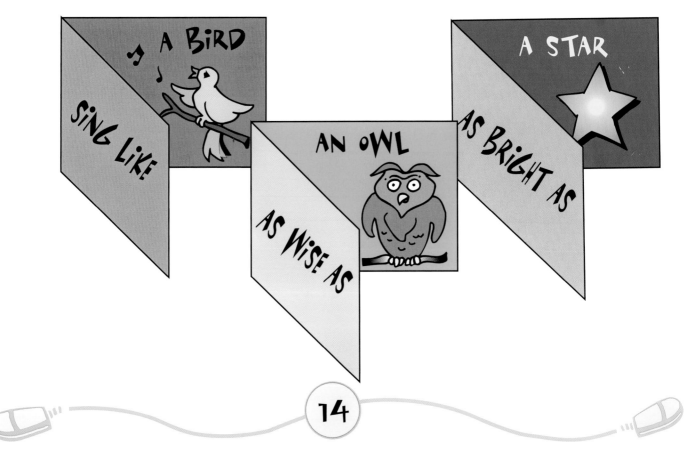

Chapter Two

Sentence Connection

Now that you've learned more about words, it's time to move on to sentences. A sentence is a group of words that makes a whole thought. These activities will help you put together some great sentences!

WRITING Funky Flip Books

A simple sentence is made up of two parts—the subject and the action. The subject is the person or thing that the sentence is telling you about, and the action is what that subject is doing. In the sentence "Sam ate," *Sam* is the subject and *ate* is the action. Easy, right? But most sentences are not simple sentences. Most sentences have more parts than a subject and an action. Many sentences also have an object. The object is the person or thing that receives the action. For instance, add the words *the cereal* to the sentence above. Now you know what Sam (the subject) ate. The cereal was eaten by Sam. Make a fun flip book of different subjects, actions, and objects so that you can create all kinds of interesting sentences.

Steps:

1 Think of some cool creatures as the subjects for your sentences.

2 Remember that you need to write the word *the* before the subject (unless the subject is a *proper name*, like *Sarah*, or a *pronoun*, like *I* or *he*). Here are some ideas for subjects to get you started: *the hippo, the space alien, Frankenstein, the clown, the teacher, the great white shark.*

3 Go into the **Paint** program. Click on the **A icon** and create a text box at the bottom of the screen. Type in one of your subjects. Remember, this is the beginning of your sentence, so you need to capitalize the first letter of the first word.

4 Using the **Paint** tools, draw a picture of your subject at the left of the screen, next to your word or words.

5 **Save** your subject and **Print** it out. (Make sure your page is set for **Landscape.**)

6 Repeat steps 2 through 4 to make other subjects.

7 Now come up with some interesting actions. Here are a few examples: *hit, threw, played, read, watched, chewed, kicked, typed.* Make sure that all of the actions are in the same *tense.* That means that they all take place in either the present (like the word *plays*) or the past (like the word *played*).

8 Using the **A icon,** type your actions the same way you typed your subjects, with each one on a new screen. It's pretty hard to draw an action, so don't worry about drawing pictures for the actions. Make as many actions as you made subjects. **Save** each word and **Print** it out before you make new ones.

9 Now think of some objects. You can use any silly words you think of to make funny endings to the sentences. Remember to write the word *the* before the objects. These are some ideas: *the pants, the caterpillars, the pepperoni, the telephone, the alligator, the grocery store.*

10 Using the **A icon,** type your objects, each on a new screen. Since this is the end of the sentence, make sure you type a period after the last word. With the **Paint** tools, draw pictures of the objects. Make as many objects as you made subjects and actions. **Save** each one and **Print** it out before you make new ones.

11 Now cut each subject, action, and object into strips of about the same size. It's okay if the strips of paper with the action words have more blank space since they don't have pictures. When you're finished cutting all the words, get a big, blank sheet of paper. Glue one subject along the top of the paper, one action in the middle, and one object along the bottom.

12 Then put the rest of your subject strips together in a neat pile and staple them together on the left side. Now place the stack of subjects on top of the subject that you already glued to the big piece of paper. Staple the subjects to the piece of paper, again on the left side, so that you can flip through them easily on the right side. Now do the same for the action strips and the object strips. See the art at right for help.

13 Now flip the strips to make lots of different sentences!

This is the question that magazine and newspaper reporters ask. They need to get straight to the point! That's what newswriting is all about—getting the important information across as quickly and clearly as possible. When reporters write a story, they try to answer a few basic questions (who, what, when, where, why, and how) as simply as possible. Try writing a short news story yourself to master the skill of these simple sentences.

Steps:

1 First, you need something to write about. So go find your story! It can be something in your home, like your cat just had kittens. Or maybe your friend just got a new baby brother or sister. There's always something interesting happening, so look around until you find the story that *you* think makes good news!

2 Once you choose your news story, it's time to report it! Click **Microsoft Works**, then **TaskWizards**, then **Common Tasks**. You'll see something called **Newsletter**. Click it twice. You might get a message asking you a question. Click "Yes, run the TaskWizards." Then you'll see three choices. Click **One Column**, then click **Create It!**

3 Highlight the word *Newsletter* and type the name of your paper over it. You can name your newsletter for the town you live in if you want to write about different local events. You can also make it a family newsletter, and just name it after your family. It's up to you!

4 Now type in your name as the reporter, since that's what you are! Type it over the words or numbers in the box below the name of the newsletter.

PSST!

If you're using a different word-processing program, then you won't be able to do this activity exactly as described. Explore your word-processing program until you find a similar way to make a newsletter.

5 Now think of a headline for your story. Type it over the words in the next box, below where you typed your name. Then click onto the text below that box. It's time to type in your news story. Remember that you have to answer the big questions in journalism: who, what, where, when, why, and how. Here's a sample news story that answers all of these questions.

North Arlington Newsletter

by David Sidney

New Garden Brings Spring Flowers

My mother planted a new garden. She spent all day Saturday digging and planting the seeds in our backyard. She wasn't alone the whole time—she dragged me and my brother outside to help in the afternoon. She said that she planted the garden because she wants flowers in the spring.

Five Kittens Born!

Mrs. Kern's cat, April, welcomed five new kittens into the world on Monday. The kittens are black with white paws.

Who? *My mother* What? *Planted a new garden*
Where? *In our backyard* When? *Saturday*
Why? *Because she wants flowers in the spring*
How? *With help from me and my brother*

6 Add pictures to your story too. Hit the **Enter** key after the end of your story a few times so that there is space between the end of the story and the next headline box. Then insert clip art that matches your story. You can change the size of the art to fit your page. Click on your art so that a box forms around it. See the dots on the box? Move the cursor over a dot on one of the corners of the box until you see the word **Resize**. Hold down your mouse button and move your mouse to change the size! You can also move the art on the page. Click **Format**, then **Text Wrap**, then **Absolute**.

7 Fill up your newsletter with several stories. Write each one the same way you wrote the first one, answering all the basic questions. You can add more clip art too if you want.

8 When you're happy with your newsletter, **Save** it and **Print** it out.

COOL IDEA!

Start a neighborhood newsletter with your friends. All of you can report your own stories!

WRITING Punctuation Plaza

The order of the words isn't the only thing that matters in forming a sentence. *Punctuation,* like periods and commas and question marks, is really important for writing good sentences. Here's a way to learn punctuation while you make your own comics!

Steps:

1 Go into the **Paint** program.

2 First, with the **Paint** tools, draw a person's face, with eyes, a nose, and a mouth. Then click on the **Ellipse** tool, and draw a large balloon shape right next to the face. You know how the conversations of comic book characters appear in balloon shapes? Use the **Pencil** tool to draw a line from the balloon shape to the face.

3 Click the **A icon** and make a text box inside the balloon shape. Pretend you're making a comic strip, and write a sentence in the balloon that a character might say; for example, *I like going to the movies.* **Save** and **Print** your sentence and picture.

4 Add and change words in your sentence to show that the character is *really* excited about movies. End the sentence with an exclamation point instead of a period. Exclamation points show excitement; for instance, *I absolutely love going to the movies!* **Save** and **Print** your excitement sentence.

5 Erase that sentence, and type in a third sentence. This time you want the character to ask someone else if he or she likes movies. In order to make a sentence into a question, you have to end it with a question mark; for example, *Do you like going to the movies?* **Save** and **Print** your question.

6 Repeat step 2 to make a new person with a new balloon shape. Type a new sentence in the balloon shape that responds to one of your original sentences. Repeat steps 3 through 5 to make your new person respond to each of the original sentences. **Save** and **Print** your work.

7 Glue the pages together so that the people look like they are talking to each other in a comic strip!

8 Make more comic strips the same way you made these, with new sentences.

Doing Dialogue

When you write *dialogue* between characters in a story, there are a lot of punctuation rules to keep in mind. That's why practicing some simple dialogue sentences is a great way to work on punctuation!

Steps:

1 Remember the sentences you wrote in the last activity? Now you're going to turn them into *dialogue*. Dialogue is the words or sentences that characters say to one another in a story or play.

2 Go into the **word-processing** program. Type the first sentence from the Punctuation Plaza activity—*I like going to the movies.* Whenever people speak in a story, there are quotation marks *before* their words and *after* their words. So make sure you use quotations marks.

3 The sentence isn't over until you've said who is talking, so make sure you delete the period and put a comma inside the second quotation mark. Then tell the reader who is talking. Type a period after the person's name, since this is the end of the sentence. Here's an example:

"I like going to the movies," said Scott.

4 Even though an exclamation point or a question mark usually means the end of a sentence, it's a little different with dialogue. If you want to show excitement or if you want your character to ask a question, then the exclamation point or question mark goes *inside* the second quotation mark. For instance:

"I absolutely love going to the movies!" said Scott.

"Do you like going to the movies?" asked Scott.

5 Type out new dialogue sentences using exclamation points and question marks. You can play with the font, the color, and the size of the words if you want. Then **Save** and **Print** all of your dialogue sentences and keep them with your dialogue balloon sentences.

HINT!

Remember that exclamation points and question marks are almost always just like periods—they show the end of a sentence. But unlike periods, they don't always show the end of a sentence in dialogue. Whenever you're confused about how to punctuate dialogue, just look at the printouts from this activity as a reminder!

Chapter Three

STORY TIME

Now you're an expert with words and sentences. You've written a poem and a newsletter. You've even practiced writing dialogue. What's left? Writing stories, of course! Writing a story is a lot of fun and also a lot of work. There are so many parts of the story to think about. You can make up crazy characters and put them anywhere in the universe you want. And *you* get to decide what happens to them! Some stories are very realistic, with characters that are just like people you know. Other stories are fantasies, with aliens or unicorns or unreal events. In this chapter you'll learn all the steps to follow when writing whatever kind of story you want to create.

WRITING STELLAR SETTING

Where will the story take place? That's the first question to ask yourself. The location of a story is called its *setting.* Your story's setting can be in your own neighborhood, in an exotic country, on board a pirate ship, or even on a distant planet. The setting is also the time when the story takes place. What year is it? What season? What time of day is everything happening? Figure it out!

Steps:

1 Go into the **Paint** program.

2 Think about the setting you want for your story. With the **Paint** tools, draw things that you would find in your setting. For instance, if your setting is a beach, draw the ocean and the sand. If it's a forest, draw trees. If it's right where you live, draw a picture of your street or your house.

3 When you're happy with your art, click the **A icon** and make a text box at the bottom of the screen. Type a few sentences describing your setting. You could talk about the weather, what there is to do there, what kind of animals might be there—anything that you find interesting about your setting!

4 **Save** your setting and **Print** it out. (Make sure you're set for **Landscape!**)

My setting is the beach. It is very hot. There are beautiful shells on the sand.

WRITING ◆ COOL CHARACTERS

When you like a story a lot, it's often because you really love the characters. Think about the characters you like to read about. Then make up a character yourself. Choose a name, and think about what the character looks like and how he or she acts. This activity shows you how to make a *character web,* which will help you develop your character.

Steps:

1 Go into the **Paint** program. Click on the **Ellipse** tool.

2 Place your cursor a little to the left of the center of the screen, then hold down the mouse button and drag the cursor to draw a medium-size circle.

3 Click on the **A icon** and make a text box inside the circle. Type in the name of your character.

4 With the **Ellipse** tool, make more circles around the first circle. Fill your screen with circles. Make sure the circles are big so that you'll be able to type inside them.

5 Click on the **Straight-Line** tool. Draw lines connecting each circle to the middle circle, as shown below. You've made the outline for your character web!

6 With the **A icon,** type important things about your character in each of the circles. You can use adjectives to describe the character *(goofy, short, smart, strong)* or write about what the character likes, has, or does *(eats anchovy pizza, owns a new bike, knows karate)*.

7 When you're finished, **Save** and **Print** your character web. Make sure your page is set for **Landscape**.

COOL iDEA!

Draw a picture of your character to go with your character web!

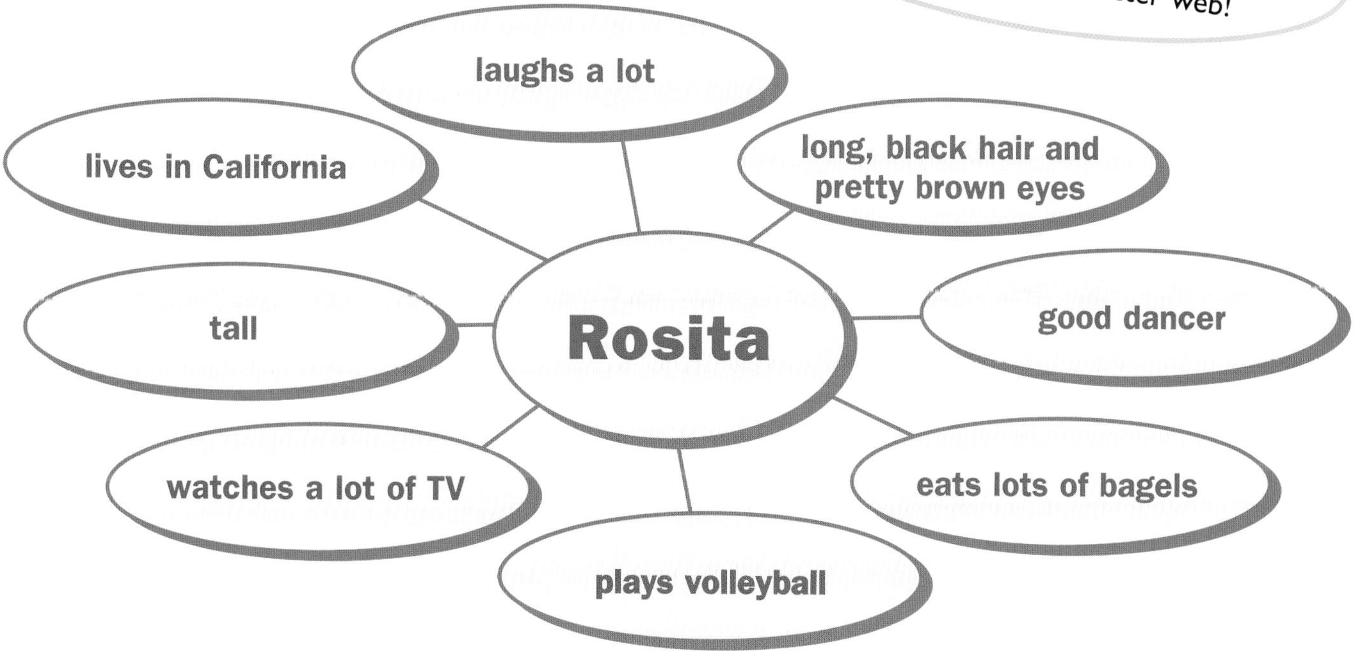

laughs a lot

lives in California

long, black hair and pretty brown eyes

tall

Rosita

good dancer

watches a lot of TV

eats lots of bagels

plays volleyball

WRITING — BEGINNING TO END

Every story has a beginning, a middle, and an end. This order, or *sequence of events,* is really important. Why? The story can only make sense if everything happens in order. Start out by making a four-sentence story cube to show how a story goes from beginning to end.

Steps:

1 Go into the **Paint** program.

2 Think of a simple story that you can explain in four sentences, like the story of a girl going to school in the morning. With the **Paint** tools, draw a picture of the first thing that happens in your story, like the girl eating breakfast.

3 Click on the **A icon,** and make a text box above the picture you drew. Type a sentence describing your picture, starting with the word *First,* like, *First, Jacky ate breakfast.* **Save** your picture and sentence and **Print** them out. Remember to make sure your computer is set for **Landscape.**

First, Jacky ate breakfast.

4 Now, on a new screen draw a picture of the next thing that happens, like leaving the house.

5 With the **A icon,** type a sentence describing this picture, starting with the word *Next,* like, *Next, Jacky left her house.* **Save** your picture and sentence and **Print** them out.

Next, Jacky left her house.

6 On a new screen draw a picture of the next thing that would happen, like getting on the school bus. With the **A icon,** type a sentence describing this picture, starting with the word *Then,* like, *Then, Jacky got on the school bus.* **Save** your picture and sentence and **Print** them out.

7 Now draw your last picture on another new screen. Draw the last thing that would happen, like arriving at school.

8 With the **A icon,** type a sentence describing the picture, starting with the word *Finally,* like, *Finally, Jacky arrived at school.* **Save** your picture and sentence and **Print** them out.

9 Now get a square tissue box. (Other small boxes would work too!) Cut out the pictures and captions, and tape or glue each to one side of the box—*in order!* You can also create art to decorate the top and bottom of the box if you want.

10 Read your story cube by turning the box. Now you can see why the sequence of events is important. There's no way that Jacky could arrive at school before she leaves her house. She also can't get on the school bus before she eats her breakfast at home. The sequence of events helps you make your story make sense.

WRITING — MAP IT OUT

So, you've got a super setting and a cool character, and you've learned about the importance of the sequence of events in a story. What's the next step? It's time to make a *story map.* A story map is actually a plan of how your story will go. Follow these steps to make your own story map on your computer.

Steps:

1 Go into the **Paint** program.

2 First plan your story! Think about the character and setting you created for your story, and ask yourself some questions:
- What will your character do in your setting?
- What people, animals, or other creatures will your character meet?
- What problems will your character have?

3 Click on the **Rectangle** tool. Starting at the left side of the page, hold down your mouse button and drag your mouse to create a large rectangle across your screen.

4 Click the **A icon,** and make a text box above the rectangle. Type in the word *Beginning*.

5 With the **A icon,** make a large text box in the rectangle—so large that it takes up the whole rectangle and you can write in it. Then type a description of how your story will begin. What will happen to the character first? What is interesting about this character? What does this character want to do?

BEGINNING

Frank really loves baseball. It's springtime, and he's excited to start playing on his local little league team. He and his two best friends go to the tryouts, and they all make the starting lineup!

6 When you are finished, **Save** and **Print** the *Beginning* box.

7 Erase all the text inside your rectangle with the **Delete** key. Then erase the word *Beginning* above the box. Type the word *Middle* there instead.

8 Next, make a new text box that fills up the empty rectangle. The middle of the story is where the character has *conflict,* which means that the character has a problem doing something that he wants to do. For instance, if your character wanted to play baseball, in the middle of the story he might injure himself. Then he would go to the doctor to see if the injury will heal in time for him to finish the season. Think of the problem that your character will have in the setting, and type up a brief description in the *Middle* rectangle.

9 Save and **Print** the *Middle* box.

10 Again, erase the text in the rectangle, and erase the word *Middle*. Type the word *Ending* above the rectangle. Then make another text box that fills up the rectangle. The ending of the story is where the character's problem is resolved. Think of how you want everything to end for your character. If he's trying to play baseball, for example, then maybe his arm heals and he ends up scoring the winning home run for his team! Type a brief description of how your story will end.

11 Save and **Print** the *Ending* box.

12 Now get a big piece of poster board. Glue the boxes down on the poster board in the correct order. Then use markers or strips of construction paper to make lines connecting the boxes together. Once you are finished, you can use your story map to write your story in the next activity!

PSST!

You can try to make the whole story map on one screen, but it might be hard to make all the rectangles fit. If you want to try it, here's how! Make the first rectangle all the way to the left of your screen. Then Copy it, and Paste it twice to create two more rectangles. Move the new rectangles next to the first one, so that they are in a line across your screen. Then label each rectangle and type the information inside them the same way you would if you were making them on separate screens!

BEGINNING

Frank really loves baseball. It's springtime, and he's excited to start playing on his local little league team. He and his two best friends go to the tryouts, and they all make the starting lineup!

MIDDLE

The season begins, and Frank is doing great. He even has the team record for home runs. Then he gets hurt in a game, and he has to go to the doctor to see how serious the injury is. He's scared he won't be able to play baseball anymore.

ENDING

Frank finds out it will only take a couple of weeks for his arm to heal. He's happy when he finally gets better and rejoins the team. Then, at the end of the season, he scores the winning home run and his team wins the championship!

Now it's time to bring your setting and character to life!
Use everything you've learned so far to write a story
you can show to your family and friends.

Steps:

1 Go into the **word-processing** program.

2 Look at the *Beginning* box on your story map. Think about what you wrote there. Now start to write your story. Introduce your character and setting. Show your character doing something that he or she likes to do. Look at your character web for reminders of what the character looks like, acts like, and enjoys. Show the character in your setting and interacting with other characters if it's appropriate.

3 Now look at the *Middle* box on your story map. Use what you wrote there to help you write the middle of your story. This is where the conflict begins. What happens to your character now? How does the character feel about what happens to him or her? What does he or she do about it? How do the other characters get involved in the problem?

 30

4 Finally, look at what you wrote in the *Ending* box on your story map. Describe what gets the character to this point. How does the ending happen? Where does it happen? Are other characters involved? Build up the events so that the reader is excited to learn what will happen to the character. Then end your story by showing how the conflict from the middle of the story is resolved and how the character feels.

Remember to choose your words carefully. Try to use very descriptive adjectives so that readers can actually "picture" what you're writing about in their minds. Use a thesaurus or a dictionary to find more words.

5 Once you've written your story, it's time to *proofread* it. When you proofread something, you check the spelling and grammar to make sure they are correct. Look at the questions below to help you proofread your story.

- Can you find any words that are spelled incorrectly? If you're not sure about some of the words, look them up in a dictionary. Most **word-processing** programs have a spell check right on your computer. Just click **Tools,** then **Spelling.** If the computer *does* find a misspelled word, you'll get a screen with lots of options. In one box you'll see your misspelled word. In another box you'll see a list of words you may have been trying to spell. Click the correct word, then click **Change.** If the word is the name of a person or thing that the computer doesn't recognize, click **Ignore.**

- Make sure you've written all your sentences correctly. Does the first word of each sentence start with a capital letter? Does each sentence end with the correct punctuation?

- Does each sentence have a subject and an action?

- Does your dialogue have quotation marks? Can the reader tell who is speaking?

6 Now that your story is perfect, you need to give it a title. Think of a title that tells the readers what your story is about. Now, make a title page. On a blank page, type in the title, then hit **Enter**. On the next line, type the word *by* and then your name—you're the author! To center these lines, click **Format**, then **Paragraph**. Under the word **Alignment**, click **Center**.

7 **Save** your story and **Print** out lots of copies!

COOL iDEA!

Make a book cover for your story. First, draw art to decorate the cover in the Paint program. You could also use the art you made in the "Stellar Setting" activity. Then Print out your art, and glue it to a piece of construction paper. Put all the pages of your story together with the cover on top, then staple them.

Frank's Amazing Baseball Season

by Mike Rusignola